GEMSTONES OF THE WORLD

MINING FOR EMERALDS

Published in 2018 by The Rosen Publishing Group, Inc.
29 East 21st Street, New York, NY 10010

First Edition

Editor: Theresa Morlock
Book Design: Reann Nye

Photo Credits: Cover TinaImages/Shutterstock.com; p. 4 photo-world/Shutterstock.com; p. 5 Victor Moussa/Shutterstock.com; p. 6 Jack Dagley Photography/Shutterstock.com; p. 7 Gary Ombler/Dorling Kindersley/Getty Images; p. 8 DEA / PHOTO 1/ De Agostini Picture Library/Getty Images; p. 9 W. Scott McGill/Shutterstock.com; p. 10 Walter Geiersperger/Corbis Documentary/ Getty Images; p. 11 Byjeng/Shutterstock.com; p. 12 Tarzhanova/Shutterstock.com; p. 13 By Zelfit/Shutterstock.com; p. 14 AnnaAiva/Shutterstock.com; p. 15 https://en.wikipedia.org/wiki/File:Payag,_Shah_Jahan_on_Horseback,_Folio_from_the_Shah_Jahan_Album_ca._1630,_Metmuseum.jpg; pp. 16, 22 J. Palys/Shutterstock.com; p. 17 ivan-96/DigitalVision Vectors/ Getty Images; p. 18 Albert Russ/Shutterstock.com; p. 19 Bloomberg/Getty Images; p. 20 Yellow Cat/Shutterstock.com; p. 21 ADRIAN DENNIS/AFP/Getty Images.

Cataloging-in-Publication Data

Names: Krajnik, Elizabeth.
Title: Mining for emeralds / Elizabeth Krajnik.
Description: New York : PowerKids Press, 2018. | Series: Gemstones of the world | Includes index.
Identifiers: ISBN 9781538328286 (pbk.) | ISBN 9781508164210 (library bound) | ISBN 9781538328347 (6 pack)
Subjects: LCSH: Emeralds–Juvenile literature. | Mineralogy–Juvenile literature.
Classification: LCC QE394.E5 K73 2018 | DDC 553.8'6–dc23

Manufactured in the United States of America

CPSIA Compliance Information: Batch Batch #BW18PK: For Further Information contact Rosen Publishing, New York, New York at 1-800-237-9932

CONTENTS

ONE OF THE "PRECIOUS FOUR"

Four gemstones make up the group known as the "precious four" or "big four." This group includes diamonds, rubies, sapphires, and emeralds. These gemstones are known as the precious four because of how rare, or uncommon, and popular they are. The more rare the gemstone, the more valuable it is.

Today, emeralds are some of the most valuable gemstones. They're often more rare than the other gems in the big four. However, it's now possible to make these precious gemstones in a **laboratory**.

The word "emerald" comes from the old French word *esmeralde*, which comes from the Greek word *smaragdos*, which means "green stone."

HOW DO EMERALDS FORM?

Earth's many kinds of rocks are made of different **minerals**. In the case of emeralds, the mineral is beryl. Beryl is made up of four elements found in Earth's crust: beryllium, aluminum, silicon, and oxygen. Beryl is formed when heat and pressure are applied to the elements inside **hydrothermal** veins.

Beryl in its purest form has no color. When different elements are present, different colors of beryl form. Emeralds' green color comes from the element chromium.

RED BERYL

HIDDEN GEMS

Red beryl of a high enough quality for gems has only been found in the Wah Wah Mountains in Utah. It's very rare and expensive. Red beryl gets its color from the presence of the element manganese. It used to be known as bixbite.

The beryl gemstone group includes emerald, aquamarine, golden beryl, morganite, and more. Aquamarine is formed when the element iron is present.

EMERALDS AROUND THE WORLD

Even though emeralds are one of the rarest gemstones, they can be found in a number of countries around the world. Emeralds are most commonly found in Colombia, Brazil, and Zambia. However, new **deposits** of emeralds have been found in other locations in South America, Africa, and Europe.

Emeralds from Colombia are known for being deep blue-green or "emerald green." Brazilian emeralds are yellow-green and more **transparent**. Zambian emeralds are closer in color to Colombian emeralds but have more of a bluish shade.

Emeralds are mined from host rocks. This means that emeralds grow within veins of other rocks or on the walls of cavities, which are hollow parts of rocks.

PRECIOUS PROPERTIES

Emeralds have their own special properties that make them different from other gemstones. Color is the most important property when deciding an emerald's value. Colombian emeralds, which are a dark blue-green color, are the most valuable. However, if they're too blue, they're less valuable.

Inclusions, or flaws, are very common in emeralds and other colored gemstones. They can affect gemstones' clarity and durability. Clarity refers to how clear or cloudy a stone is. Durability refers to how strong or breakable a stone is.

HIDDEN GEMS

It's very rare to find a natural emerald with no inclusions. A natural emerald with very few inclusions can cost more than a high-quality diamond of the same weight.

Inclusions mean that an emerald is natural. It is very common for natural emeralds to be treated with a green oil to fill in inclusions and make the emerald's color more **vivid**. This treatment also helps protect the emerald from chipping.

The Mohs' scale measures a mineral's hardness by its resistance to being scratched. Diamonds are the hardest mineral on the Mohs' scale with a value of 10. Emeralds can be more **fragile** because of their inclusions.

When an emerald is cut and polished, its surface reflects light like glass. This property is known as vitreous luster. Emeralds are often cut in a special shape to make the color of the stones more vivid and protect the stones from cracking.

CABOCHON EMERALDS

Gemstones that are shaped and polished but not **faceted** are known as cabochons.

POLISHED AND FACETED EMERALDS

THE HISTORY OF EMERALDS

For hundreds of years, people have wondered at the beauty and rarity of emeralds. The first known emerald mines were in Egypt. These mines were in operation from about 330 BC to well into the 18th century. Egyptian queen Cleopatra is said to have had a love of emeralds, which can be seen in the jewelry she wore.

The Inca people of South America also used emeralds in their jewelry. Emeralds had a special place in Inca religion.

HIDDEN GEMS

When the Spanish arrived in South America, they were in search of precious metals. They traded emeralds for gold and silver.

During the 1600s, emeralds from Colombia were shipped to India. Emperor Shāh Jahān, pictured here, had religious writings carved into emeralds and wore them.

FOLKLORE AND MYTHS

Many **cultures** have **folklore** and myths connected to emeralds. The ancient Egyptians believed emeralds had special powers. Some believed that emeralds could help treat eye diseases. One belief held that if the dead were buried with emeralds, they would remain young in the afterlife.

People from other cultures believed that emeralds gave their owner the ability to see into the future if they put an emerald under their tongue. Emeralds were also said to reveal the truth and protect the wearer against evil spells.

Some religious writings say Solomon, the king of Israel from around 970 to 931 BC, had a powerful magic ring. Some writings say this ring had four small gemstones, one of which was an emerald.

FIND YOUR OWN EMERALDS

Finding your own emerald could be just a road trip away. The Emerald Hollow Mine in Hiddenite, North Carolina, is the only emerald mine in the United States where the public can go **prospecting** for their own treasure.

The Crabtree Emerald Mine in Little Switzerland, North Carolina, is where businesses such as the Tiffany Company used to get some of their emeralds. This mine was active from 1895 to the 1990s. People must have a permit to go prospecting at this mine.

HIDDENITE

HIDDEN GEMS

You can find other hidden gems at Emerald Hollow Mine, including aquamarines, sapphires, amethysts, and quartz crystals. A rare gemstone called hiddenite can also be found there.

You don't need to go all the way to Colombia to find an emerald. At the Emerald Hollow Mine, you can even turn any emeralds you find into a piece of jewelry.

FAMOUS EMERALDS

Some of the world's largest emeralds have been named and are now on display in museums. Many are left uncut to prevent them from cracking. The Guinness Emerald Crystal is a 12.4-ounce (351.5 g) uncut emerald. This emerald was found in the Cosquez mines in Colombia.

Some emeralds have been made into beautiful works of art. The Sacred Emerald Buddha is an 18.48-ounce (523.9 g) emerald statue. It was carved from an emerald crystal that weighed 25.4 ounces (720.1 g).

HIDDEN GEMS

Emerald is the birthstone for people born in May. It's also the gem for people's 20th and 35th wedding anniversaries.

This 17th-century emerald wine cup was sold for more than $2.3 million dollars in 2003.

GREEN WITH ENVY

Emeralds are shining natural wonders of our world. Without the right surroundings, these lovely gems would never form. Throughout history, emeralds have been prized for their beauty. Some people even believed them to have magic powers.

Although they are stunning, emeralds can be very expensive and make you green with envy. Synthetic, or fake, emeralds can be made in a laboratory, which makes them more affordable. Someday, you may own one yourself!

GLOSSARY

culture: The beliefs and way of life of a certain group of people.

deposit: An amount of matter built up naturally in the earth.

facet: To cut small, flat surfaces on a gem to make it more shiny and beautiful. Also, the flat surfaces themselves.

folklore: Ideas or stories that may not be true but that many people have heard or read.

fragile: Easily broken or hurt.

hydrothermal: Of or relating to hot water.

laboratory: A room or building in which people do scientific experiments and tests.

mineral: A naturally occurring solid substance that is not of plant or animal origin.

prospect: To explore, especially for mineral deposits.

transparent: Clear enough or thin enough to see through.

vivid: Very strong or bright.

INDEX

WEBSITES

Due to the changing nature of Internet links, PowerKids Press has developed an online list of websites related to the subject of this book. This site is updated regularly. Please use this link to access the list: www.powerkidslinks.com/gotw/emer